Better Homes and Gardens

Pattern Adjustments

BETTER HOMES AND GARDENS BOOKS
NEW YORK   DES MOINES

Better Homes and Gardens Creative Sewing Library
© Meredith Corporation, 1966. All Rights Reserved.
Printed in the United States of America.
Third Printing.
Library of Congress Catalog Card Number: 66-8592.
SBN: 696-01205-7

CREATIVE SEWING

Beautiful fabrics and exciting pattern styles make sewing more rewarding than ever. With today's new techniques and equipment, sewing can be fun for the beginner as well as the accomplished seamstress.

Better Homes and Gardens Creative Sewing Library presents sewing methods based on common sense—practical, professional tips that show how to give clothes for the whole family a "custom-made" look.

The Creative Sewing Library has been prepared under the guidance of Miss Lucille Rivers, one of America's eminent sewing experts. To help women learn the easy, professional methods of sewing she describes in the books, she has drawn upon her long experience in the field. Miss Rivers has directed her own custom salon in New York, and she has served as consultant to many leading clothing manufacturers.

She has created new styles for fashion shows, and has lectured on sewing in department stores in this country, Australia, and New Zealand. For many years Miss Rivers was sewing editor of NBC's popular "Home Show," and she has conducted sewing demonstrations on many other television programs. In the Creative Sewing Library, she shares her fashion knowledge and dressmaking experience with you.

Titles in the Creative Sewing Library are:
Professional Sewing Tips
How to Sew for Children
Pattern Adjustments
Tailoring Suits and Coats
Sewing Casual Clothes

CONTENTS

The commercial pattern

The commercial pattern is a vital part of sewing equipment. Unless a woman knows how to make her own pattern, it is the only guide she has for style and size of a garment.

Pattern manufacturers provide a wealth of sewing information for you. Read your pattern envelope thoroughly, as well as the sewing instruction guide enclosed in it. The more you learn about your pattern, the greater help it will be to you.

In this book you will learn how to eliminate complicated fittings. This sewing and fitting technique is based on correct use of the commercial pattern. Generally, choose a pattern according to your bust measurement. The bodice is the most difficult to alter, so buy the size that gives you the best fit in the bust. (Later, exceptions to this rule will be explained.)

Waist and hipline are easiest to adjust, so don't be concerned if these pattern measurements are not the same as yours.

Facts about commercial patterns

All pattern companies use the same standard body measurements. These have been established by the National Bureau of Standards. A size 14 from one company has the same proportions and body ease as all other patterns in size 14.

If you wear a size 14 pattern in a dress, you also take the same size in a suit, coat, or blouse. The pattern allows all the ease necessary for proper fit and for the lining. It also allows enough ease so the suit jacket may be worn over a blouse, and a coat may be worn over another garment.

Never buy a pattern by your ready-to-wear size. There is no uniformity of size in ready-to-wear clothing. Each manufacturer sets his own sizing. Expensive clothes are usually cut large, which is why some women can wear a size 10 in one dress, and a 12 or 14 in others.

Patterns are made to fit various figure types. You can buy patterns for misses, women's, half-size, junior, teen-age, sub-teen, and girls' figure types. You'll see the importance of buying your pattern in the correct figure type as you read the instructions for pattern adjustments.

Compare your measurements with the charts on the pattern envelope to determine which figure type and pattern size will most nearly fit you.

Your sewing will be based on the commercial pattern and its use, so study these pages carefully, and become familiar with the information.

Pattern envelopes

Your pattern envelope contains the following valuable information:

1 Several views or styles that can be made from the pattern are illustrated. Decide which style you want to make. The fabric requirements are based on these views.

2 Generally, a diagram of the number and shape of the pattern pieces is shown on the envelope back.

3 The back gives a fabric requirement chart, showing the amount needed for each view. Fabrics come in 35-36, 39, 42-44 and 50-52 inch widths. The pattern companies choose the fabric widths they consider most suitable to the style of the dress. Standard widths for various fabrics are: Cottons and linens, 35-36; silks, 39 (and sometimes 45); blended fabrics, 42-45; wools and some blends, 50-52.

4 A body measurement chart shows comparative sizes at a glance.

5 Suggested fabrics for the style are listed, as well as those that would not be suitable.

6 Notions you will need are listed, i.e. thread, buttons, zipper, etc.

7 If the style is shown in a check, stripe, or plaid, it has been especially designed for them, and will be easier to make in these designs.

8 There is also a guide for cutting and assembling your garment.

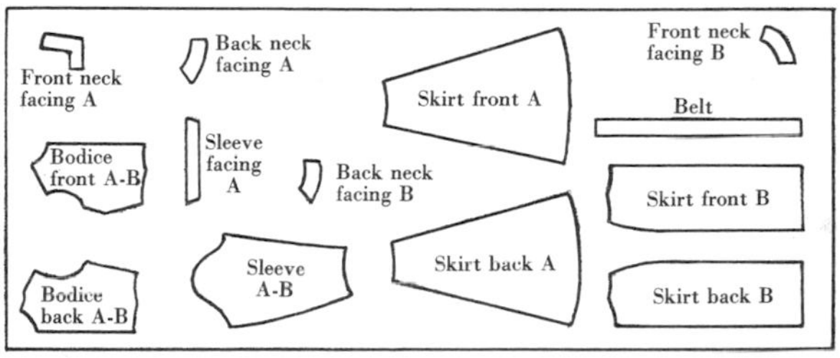

FABRIC REQUIRED	Sizes	10	12	14	16	18
VIEW A						
35″ Without Nap	Yds.	4⅞	4⅞	4⅞	5	5⅛
39″ Without Nap	Yds.	4½	4½	4½	4⅞	4⅞
45″ Without Nap	Yds.	3⅞	4	4	4¼	4¼
Skirt Lining (Optional)						
39″ Fabric	Yds.	1¾	1¾	1¾	1¾	1¾
VIEW B						
35″ Without Nap	Yds.	3¼	3⅜	3⅜	3⅞	3⅞
45″ Without Nap	Yds.	2½	2⅝	2⅞	3	3
52″ Without Nap	Yds.	2⅛	2¼	2¼	2⅜	2⅜

BODY MEASUREMENTS		10	12	14	16	18
Bust	Ins.	31	32	34	36	38
Waist	Ins.	24	25	26	28	30
Hip	Ins.	33	33	34	38	40
Back waist length	Ins.	15¾	16	16¼	16½	16¾
Finished A or B length from back of regular neckline (2-inch hem)	Ins.	44½	45	45½	45¾	46

SUGGESTED FABRICS: Linen, printed silk or cotton, synthetic mixtures, tweed, lightweight wool, jersey, crepe.
NOTE: Not suitable for diagonal prints or diagonal weaves.

NOTIONS: Thread, 12″ or 14″ dress placket zipper, wide belt; View A—ribbon seam binding; View B—Opt. ribbon binding.

The alteration pattern

Years ago, a woman was taught to take her measurements, compare them to the pattern, then adjust the pattern to these measurements before she cut the garment. In this way she was able to eliminate unnecessary fitting before the garment was even cut. It worked in theory, or when an expert took the measurements. But when a woman did her own measuring, there was too much margin for error; another method had to be devised to eliminate needless fitting.

The professional fields of ready-to-wear and pattern design helped to provide the answer.

Ready-to-wear designers assist in making the first pattern for a dress. It is made to fit the proportions of a tall, willowy, professional model who wears the dress in the showroom. Once the dress is accepted into the line, it is sent to the factory where it is recut to the manufacturer's standard size or body line.

Each manufacturer has his own master pattern or "sloper" based on his body line or standard size.

This is why women who buy ready-made clothes usually look for a particular brand name or designer. They have discovered that a size 14 in that brand fits them perfectly. Actually, they have been fortunate enough to find a manufacturer whose clothes are cut in a body line that fits them. All of the size 14 garments in this ready-to-wear brand would fit equally well, regardless of style, because they are made from the master pattern for the same proportioned figure.

This is also true with pattern companies. All patterns in one size are made to fit the same proportioned figure, regardless of style. The empire or basque-type bodice may allow only three inches of ease, while the shirt style may allow as much as five inches, but both are still made for the same figure. The style of the garment determines the difference in amount of ease allowed.

To keep this uniformity of size, all the pattern companies also work from a master pattern or "sloper." The sloper consists of a front and back bodice, a front and back skirt, and sleeve. The pattern companies

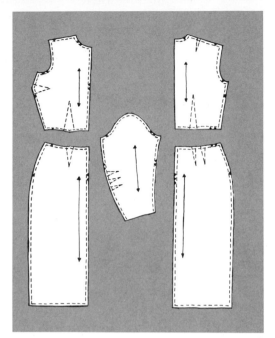

sell this master as a "Basic Pattern."

Once you learn to use this pattern, you will find that fitting has been almost entirely eliminated. With this basic pattern to work from, your fitting will simply consist of the try-on of an almost-completed dress that requires only minor adjustments.

If you have a perfectly proportioned figure with no excess weight, you can probably buy a pattern according to your bust measurement. But if your bust is larger than average, if you have gained a considerable amount of weight, or if your back has become broader through poor posture or added weight, you cannot choose your pattern by bust measurement. A pattern bought by this measurement would go around the body, but would not *fit*. The armhole and neckline would be too large, and a too-large armhole is the greatest cause of discomfort and poor appearance.

Buy the size pattern that gives you a high armhole that fits close, but does not bind. The only way to judge the right size is to try on the armhole. This sometimes means that you will have to buy several sizes of basic pat-

terns until you find the right one. Experience has shown that most women who have the figure problems just described can usually buy a pattern two sizes smaller than bust measurement.

Actually, it is bone structure and frame that determine correct pattern size. A small-boned woman, no matter how much weight she may have gained, will usually take a smaller pattern than the large-boned woman who actually measures the same in the bust. Checking the armhole sizes of the two will prove this.

To test armhole size, cut only one-half of the basic bodice pattern in muslin. Try it on. If it seems too high,

remember that seam allowances must still come off. You might turn back the seam allowance and check the finished size. If the armhole drops well below the underarm, you need a smaller size pattern.

Patterns are available in a range of sizes in several figure types—subteen, teen, girls, junior, misses, women's, and half-sizes. If you have found a type that fits you best, buy your basic pattern in that category. Adjustments cannot be transferred from one figure type pattern to another, because each one is cut for a completely different body line.

How to make the basic pattern

Cut out your basic pattern in muslin, exactly like the pattern. Sew up the darts and seams, assembling bodice and sleeves first (A). Later, when the size is correct, assemble skirt.

Make no alterations when stitching the basic muslin; it must be identical to the pattern. Baste it together, or sew with a large stitch on the sewing machine. The bodice should always be left open down the front, since it is easier to put on and fit this way. Be sure to mark the center front line. Slip bodice on with sewed darts to the outside, and pin down center front line (B).

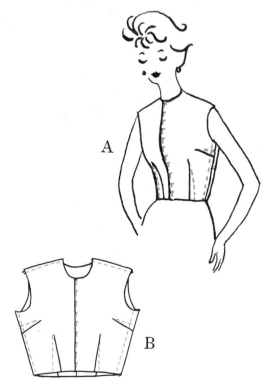

Before you fit your basic muslin, read the following information on professional fitting methods. It will help you understand the importance of posture in the fit of your clothes.

If the basic is much smaller than you measure, it may not meet at the front. Simply pin it at the neck and start to check the needed alterations.

Never alter the armhole. You have purchased your pattern in a size to give you a good fit at the armhole. If it feels tight when you first put on the muslin, it is because it needs alterations across the back. Too few women ever alter the back of a pattern, yet most of them need it. Until the back is correctly fitted, no other part of the muslin can be altered.

Adjusting a muslin

It is easier to have someone else fit the muslin on you, but it is possible for you to do it yourself.

Turn and stitch seam allowances at neck, armhole, and waist. Try on the muslin. Pin the front closed, if possible, and check side waist length.

Remove the muslin and lengthen or shorten it across the back only. (See next page). Try on the muslin again. Check the back shoulder width by bringing your arms forward. Check to see if underarm seam pulls toward the back. If the back needs widening, remove muslin and slash each side of the back from the shoulder to waist. (See next page.) Pin the shoulder dart in deeper. The wider back is also usually more rounded. Darts will be sewed in later. Pin the shoulder seams. Try on the muslin again. The armhole and underarm seams should be correct.

If the bodice fronts need enlarging, you can adjust by measurement, as described on page 14. You can make any other necessary front adjustments in front of a mirror.

Fitting the back muslin

To fit the back muslin, first check the length of the back waist. This measurement is always checked at the side seam. Turn back a generous seam allowance at the waistline. This is the only point where you can determine whether it is the waist length that needs to be altered.

If the side back waist is too long, shorten the muslin across the entire back the same amount shortened at the side. This is vitally important—

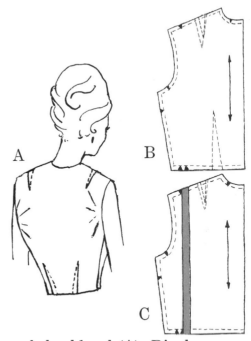

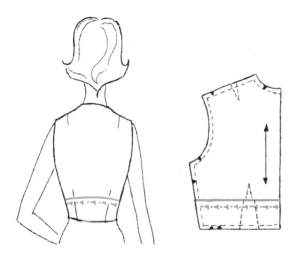

sometimes the center back will still seem too long, even after the alteration has been made. This indicates a posture fault that must be corrected by an adjustment across the shoulders, rather than additional adjustment at the waistline. Leave this alteration, for the moment; you will see how and why the adjustment across the shoulder gives a better fit.

Full back

Next, check the back of the muslin. If the back seems tight across the shoulder, and there is a ripple at the armhole, this indicates that you are round-shouldered (A). Ripples occur at the armhole because the back needs more fitting than the shoulder dart provides. Rip the shoulder seam from armhole toward neck and refit the dart, making it deeper and longer until the back of the armhole fits flat and smooth (B). Re-pin the shoulder seam. If the front shoulder seam is wider, leave it as it is for the moment.

The back shoulders will now be too narrow. Check the side seam at the waistline to see if it pulls toward the back. If so, slash from the waistline up through the shoulder, close to the armhole. Spread from shoulder to waistline. Insert a strip of fabric and pin in place (C), allowing space needed down the back. Be sure to allow enough at the shoulder for comfort across back, plus an armhole seam. If more must be added at the waistline, spread the muslin so that the side seam is at the underarm where it belongs, then pin in place.

When you make an adjustment in

your muslin, remember that it will eventually be applied to the paper pattern, which must lay flat. In adjusting the back, piecing could be wider at the waist and taper to the shoulder, or wider at the shoulder and taper to the waist. It must taper gradually, just as if you were working with paper.

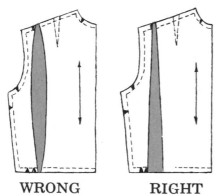

WRONG   RIGHT

Often, your pattern size seems too small because the back is tight across the shoulders, although the rest of the pattern fits properly. You need only to broaden the shoulders for a comfortable fit.

To make an adjustment, slash across under the armhole and up through the shoulder, moving this piece out on the shoulder to give the necessary fullness across the back (A). The back shoulder must be made broader because the figure is round-shouldered. Extra fullness is needed across the shoulder blades but not at the top of the shoulder. To make back and front shoulders fit, it is usually necessary to make a dart

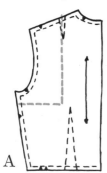

A   B

at the back shoulder. This takes up the extra fabric so front and back shoulder seams are even (B), and gives a better fit to the rounded back.

Check the waist length again at the side seam. *Whatever corrections were made at the side seam must also be made across the entire back of the muslin.* Now you're ready to make the final corrections on the back. If these alterations are necessary, make them across back of shoulder from armhole seam to armhole seam. They're usually needed because of posture.

Round back

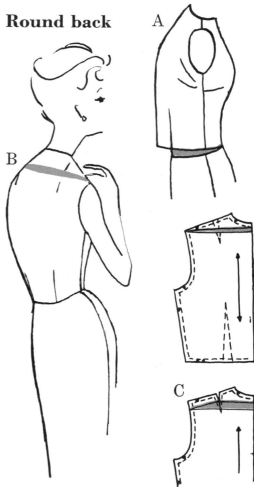

If the muslin droops on either side toward the armhole, or the back waistline seems too short at the center back (A), slash the back from under the back neck across toward each armhole. Open the necessary amount, insert a piece of fabric, and pin into place (B). When more than one-half inch is needed, the figure is generally very round-shouldered and needs more fitting to correct.

Adjust pattern only by slashing through the center of the shoulder dart and spread as shown (C). This makes the back longer, and gives a deeper dart which shapes the shoulders to the more rounded back.

Too-erect figure

With this figure, the muslin usually has a fold under the back neck or a droop between the shoulder blades. The back waistline is also too long at the center back (A). To eliminate this length, pin a dart under the back neckline, tapering to nothing toward the armholes (B). Make the same adjustment in the pattern (C).

The dart also eliminates the fullness across the shoulders which is causing the droop.

Fitting the front muslin

After the back has been enlarged, many women find that the front of the muslin fits very well. The muslin will feel much more comfortable because it is shaped to the contour of your own body. The too-narrow back can distort the fit of the front and also cause the sleeve to feel too tight and bind the upper arm. A surprising number of problems will disappear when the back is enlarged.

Full-busted figure

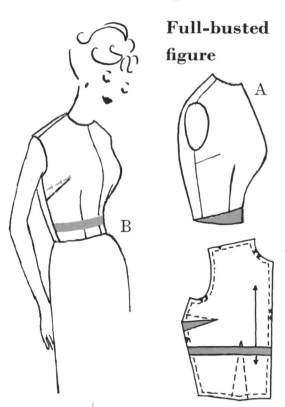

If the waistline is the correct length at the back and the sides, but is short in front directly under the bustline, the bodice requires more cupping for the bust than the pattern allows (A).

Cut along the alteration line and

lengthen the front waist the necessary amount. Be sure it's the same directly across the front. Pin a piece of fabric there. At the bust dart, take in the amount added to the front length, making the dart deeper (B). This will give more cupping for the full bust, and since nothing has been done to the back and sides, the seams will be even. When pinning the side seam dart, shape it toward the bust with the end of the dart about 1 inch from the point of the bust.

Make the entire dart higher or lower, if needed. Be sure that the bust darts run upward to give a younger and more youthful lift to the bustline for the full-busted figure.

Flat-chested figure

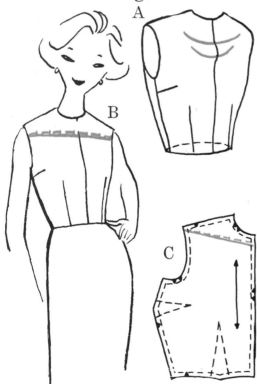

Usually with this figure fault, the front waistline is too long and it droops at the center front (A). Eliminate the extra length by taking a dart from under the neckline, taper-

ing it to nothing toward the armhole (B). Make the same adjustment in the pattern piece (C).

Full-busted, flat-chested

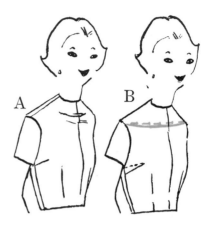

As the full-busted type figure grows round-shouldered, the chest becomes flatter (A). Follow instructions for a full-busted figure, lengthening muslin in the front and taking up the dart. Then alter just as for a flat-chested figure (B). Transfer alterations to pattern at same points (C) for a good fit.

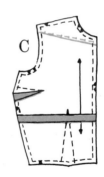

Very full bust

The figure with a very full bustline needs a special alteration, but it can be adjusted by working from measurements. After the back has been adjusted, measure from side seam to side seam across the front at the waist and bust. Be sure to take this measurement over the fullest part of the bust. (If bustline is lower than on the pattern, rip out upper part of waistline dart and reshape it so that

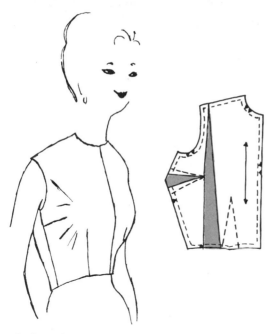

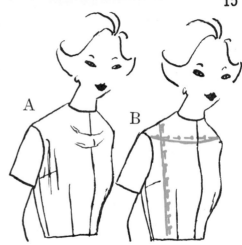

it is 1 inch below the point of bust.)

Mark a line from side seam toward point of bust to indicate the new mark for the bustline dart (dart must also be lowered). Add 1 inch for ease to the measurement across the bust. Divide the bust and waist measurement in half, which gives the amount to be added to each bodice front.

Slash muslin from waist to shoulder between waist dart and side seam. Slash across side dart. Spread muslin at bust and waist the amount that is shown in your measurements. Side dart opens automatically. Insert and sew fabric where muslin is slashed to enlarge it. Re-pin the side dart where re-marked. Pin underarm seams.

Try on muslin. It will now fit across front. Refit bust dart, if necessary.

Small-busted figure

The amount of fullness over the bustline is more than is needed for this figure (A). If the shoulders are narrow as well, take a tuck from the top of the shoulder straight down toward the waistline, eliminating the extra fullness (B). If the shoulders are nor-

mal, and only the bustline has to be made smaller, a dart can be fitted from waistline up to notch at front armhole of the muslin. Transfer these same alterations to your pattern (C).

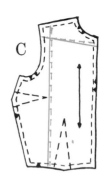

A figure that is both small-busted and flat-chested requires a combination of alterations. Fit the same dart used to adjust for the flat-chested figure to eliminate the extra length at the front waistline. Follow the instructions above to correct for the small bust. Make the same corrections in the pattern.

Too-wide shoulders

If the shoulders are too wide (A), fold a tuck from top of shoulder along side of the armhole, tapering to nothing toward the bust. *Tuck should be the same width from the shoulder to the armhole notch, taper-*

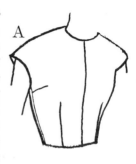

16

the top of the armhole will hit your shoulder first and the neck will be too high (A). This extra fabric will droop and the front of the dress will seem to sag (B). The dart used across the front will change the slope of the shoulders to fit yours, and the dress will hang correctly (C). If a fold forms under the back neckline, use the same adjustment there.

Sloping shoulders

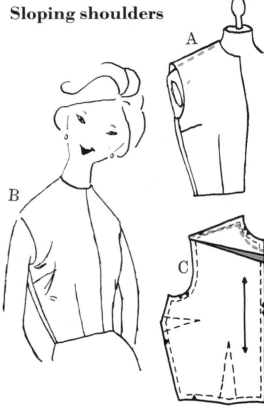

ing to nothing below that point (B). Mark and fold into the pattern in the same way (C).

Square shoulders

If your shoulders are more square than the pattern allows, you will find that when you put on your muslin,

If the shoulder of your garment fits at the neck, but not at the top of the arm (A), or if fabric droops, causing folds to form under the arm and along the armhole seams (B), slash from under the neck toward the armhole to correct (C). Notice that all adjustments are done within the basic pattern to insure keeping the correct armhole and neckline.

Decreasing the waistline

Before adjusting the waistline for

size on your muslin, check the under-arm seamline. It should be straight up and down, pulling neither to front nor back. If the waistline is too big,

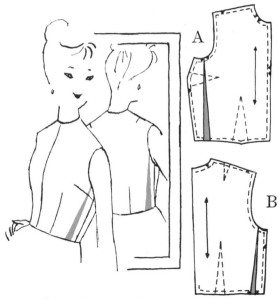

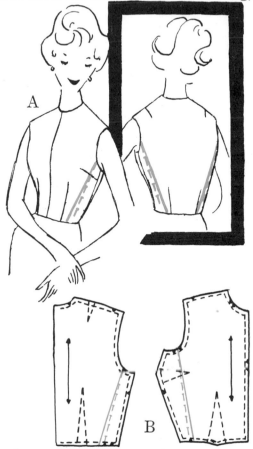

take a dart on both the back and front bodice from waistline toward armhole, to give a snug fit (A). Pin the dart in back and front bodice pieces at the same points. The dart shapes toward the armhole but does not alter the armhole size (B).

Increasing the waistline

To increase waistline, slash from waist toward armhole and insert the amount needed in both front and back. Amount added is not always same in front and back bodice pieces.

For instance, if the underarm seam of the bodice pulls toward the front, it means that the front of the figure

protrudes and the increase in size should be made only on front waist.

To make this alteration, slash your basic pattern from waistline to arm-hole, and insert the amount of fabric needed at the front to correct the underarm seam (A).

If the back is more full, the seam will pull toward the back. Adjust this the same way (B).

Too-long waistline

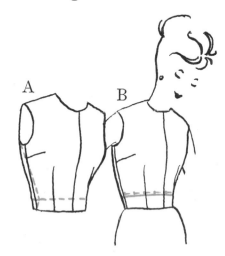

If the waistline is too long all around, shorten by pinning a tuck across front and back, between bust and the waistline. Pattern usually shows where line should be. Depth of tuck will be same front and back (B). Adjust pattern here.

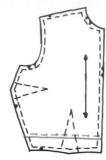

Too-short waistline

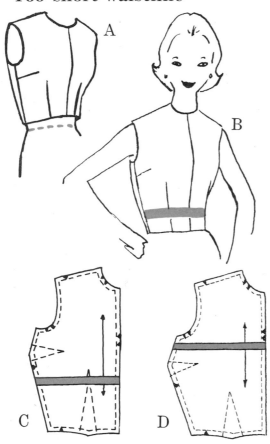

If your muslin is too short in the waist (A), lengthen it by cutting along the alteration line and inserting fabric (B). Then make the pattern adjustment by cutting it at the same point. Insert tissue to make pattern the correct length (C).

When front waist has to be lengthened, and side dart has to be lowered, it is easier to lengthen the bodice above the bust dart, taking care of both adjustments at once (D).

Full bust, small waistline

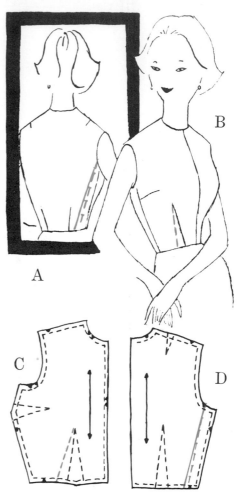

With the small waistline and the full bust, the waist adjustment can also be used to give a better bust fit. The back waistline is made smaller by taking a dart at the side of the waist, from the waistline toward the armhole (A). Make the front part of the waistline smaller by taking a deeper waistline dart. Fit the dart on the outside edge of the dart line (B). On the pattern, mark the front dart deeper only on the outside line of the dart, so that bodice and skirt darts will line up (C). Alter the back like the muslin (D). Never take back darts in deeper; the back bodice will appear to bulge, the figure will look round-shouldered.

Fitting the skirt

Baste the muslin skirt to the fitted bodice and begin your fitting. This may mean some "putting on and taking off" which can be a little tedious, but remember that you will have to do it only once. Then your fitting problems will be over!

If you decided the smaller size muslin bodice was better for you, then, regardless of how the skirt fits, use the same size skirt pattern. It is less confusing to work with the same size pattern for the entire garment. The bodice will give a better fit, and the skirt is easy to adjust.

Matching bodice and skirt darts

The darts toward the center on the front and back bodice should always form a continuous line. This is why the darts should be taken in or let out only on the outside line.

Fitting for the small hip

When the waist and hips are both smaller than the pattern, a tuck can be taken the whole length of the muslin, and folded into the pattern at the same point (A and B).

When only the hips are smaller and need adjusting, fit out the excess fullness at the side seam of the muslin. You can fold this same amount off the pattern before it is cut, or you can fit it out and leave it in the seam of the finished garment.

If the front or back of the skirt has a puff below the darts that can't be fitted out, the darts are too deep, giving more shaping than is needed (C). Refit the darts, making them smaller by letting out on the dart.

Remove the excess from the waist and hip size by taking a tuck the length of the muslin. Correct the pattern in the same way (D).

Generally, this adjustment is needed only in the back, except when the stomach is also flat. In that case, further adjustment will be necessary.

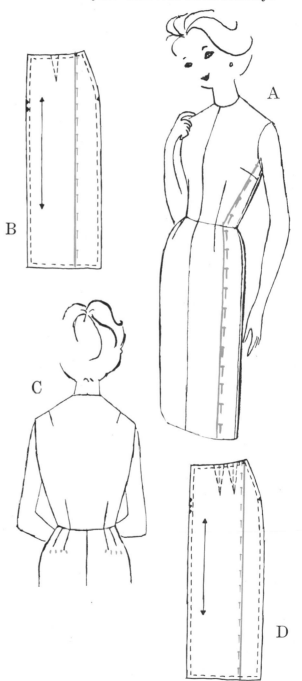

Fitting for the full hip

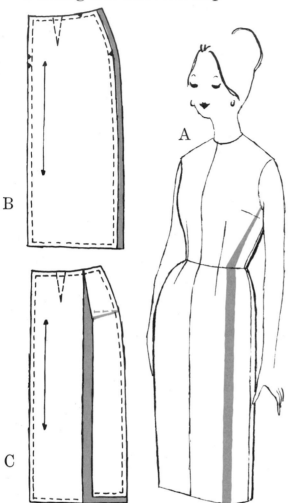

dart across the side skirt at the fullest part of the hip. Taper the dart from nothing at the side seam toward the slash to shape the skirt.

Make the same adjustment in the pattern (C) as on the muslin.

Increasing the waistline

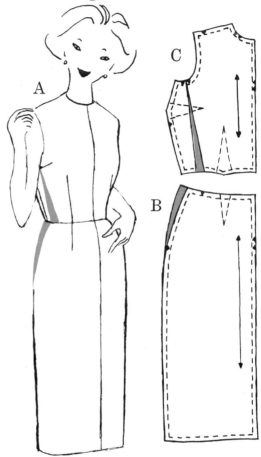

When the hips are wider than the pattern size, let out the seams of your muslin and, when cutting your dress, add the necessary amount at the same places. If a large amount has to be added at the hipline and not at the waistline, the muslin can be slashed from the hem to the waist about 4 inches in from the side seam. Spread the muslin the amount needed for the correct hip size and pin a piece of fabric here to hold (A).

To adjust pattern, add the same amount at side seam (B). Amount spread at fullest part of hip should be the same as at the hemline.

To remove the extra flare, pin a

Increase the skirt waist size by adding at the side seam of the muslin or pattern (A and B). Never slash the skirt to adjust the waist size as is sometimes done to alter the bodice waistline (C).

Increase the skirt waist size by the same amount and at the same point as the bodice waistline was increased; that is, on the front skirt piece only, on the back skirt piece only, or on both front and back pieces.

Decreasing the waistline

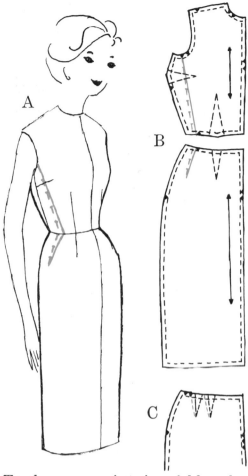

to sag and look round-shouldered.

Sway-back

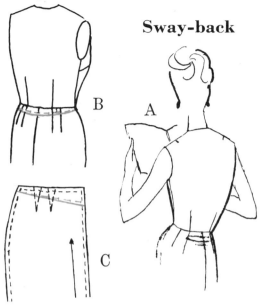

To decrease waist size, fold a dart from the waistline toward the hip. Alter the skirt the same amount as the bodice (A and B). If the waist is very small in proportion to the hips, alter the skirt back waist by making fitting darts slightly deeper. Adjust the darts only on the side toward the side seam, never on the side toward the center back (C). Do not make the skirt front fitting darts deeper, except when fitting for large pelvic bones. Altering bodice darts is exactly the reverse. The front darts of the bodice can be made deeper to give a better fit to the bust when making the waistline smaller, but back darts are never made deeper, as this would make the figure appear

Usually with this figure fault, folds appear across the top of the skirt just below the waistline (A). Pin the fold across the top of the skirt, tapering it to nothing at either side so that it fits correctly (B). Check the grain line, making sure it runs evenly around the fullest part of the hips. Make the adjustment in your pattern at the same point (C).

High abdomen

With this fault, the skirt rides up at center front (A). To correct, open the skirt at the center-front waist-

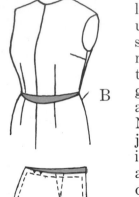

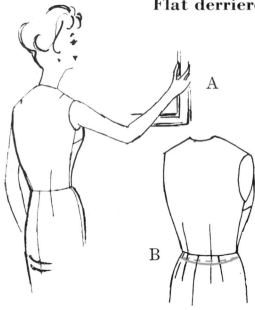

line, and drop it until skirt hangs smoothly (B). It may be necessary to add fabric to give more length at waistline seam. Now make the adjustment by adding the necessary amount to the top of the skirt pattern to correct for this figure fault, giving a good fit at the waist (C).

Flat derriere

When the figure is flat in back, the amount of shaping needed for the full derriere is not necessary (A). To eliminate it, open the back darts and make smaller. Pin the excess fabric out at the side seams. Sometimes with this figure, the skirt also has a tendency to sag at the back. This can be eliminated by fitting a dart across the top of the skirt under the waistline, as for the sway-back figure (B). To adjust the pattern, re-mark the back darts, making them smaller. Fold the dart across the pattern under the waistline as you do for the sway-back figure (C). To remove the excess fullness across the muslin skirt, pin a tuck the length of the skirt close to the side seam.

Large pelvic bone

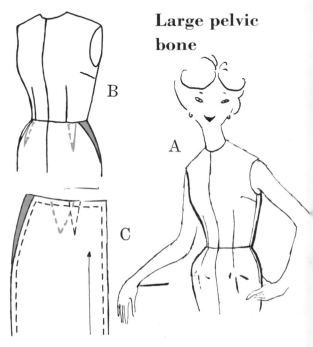

This is almost exclusively a fault of the junior figure. The hipbone protrudes, causing a bad fit at the side seam and waistline of skirt (A). Take a dart from the waistline toward the hipbone. If the front skirt has a dart, move it nearer the side seam so that it fits over hipbone. Then make it deeper so the fit is smooth. This may mean enlarging the front waistline, which is done by adding extra fabric at the waist seams (B). To adjust the pattern, re-mark the waistline darts at the correct point. If the waist size has to be increased, add the extra amount needed onto the outside waist seams of the pattern (C).

Sleeves

Now you are ready to baste the sleeves into the bodice and check the fit. If there are three darts in the sleeve, the center dart should come at the point of the elbow when the arm is bent. If there is just a single dart, as in the three-quarter sleeve, the point of the dart should be toward the point of the elbow.

If a dart is too high on the arm, slash across the upper sleeve and lengthen it so the darts are at the correct point on the arm. The sleeve forearm can then be lengthened or shortened according to arm length.

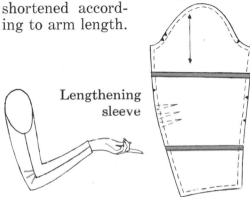

Lengthening sleeve

If the darts are below the elbow, take a tuck across the upper part of the sleeve to shorten it. Lengthen or shorten the sleeve forearm for your proper arm length.

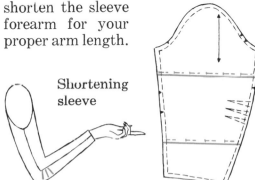

Shortening sleeve

If the elbows are exceptionally pointed, even though darts are in the right place, sleeves may feel too tight and pull from shoulders. More elbow room is needed. To check, pin each dart a little deeper and test by bending the elbow. When it feels comfortable, measure the amount added to the dart. When adjusting the sleeve pattern, slash through the center of the darts toward the inside sleeve seam and spread each dart the necessary amount. The darts are deeper when sewed and give more cupping at the elbow for a more comfortable sleeve. If the sleeve was lengthened or shortened, adjust the pattern at the same points as on the muslin.

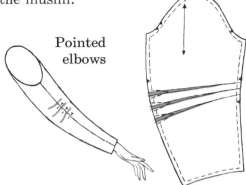

Pointed elbows

The figure with a full upper arm usually needs more fullness at the top of the sleeve, but not a larger armhole. To increase sleeve size without increasing armhole size, slash length of the sleeve through the center, and spread the required amount. When adjusting pattern, slash the length of sleeve and spread. Take darts from the slash toward the cap of the sleeve to make it lie flat. Darts taper to nothing at the armhole and do not affect the armhole size.

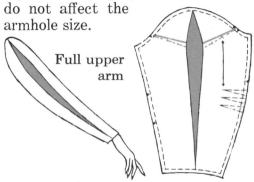

Full upper arm

Adjustments for special types

Princess line

Lengthening and shortening waist

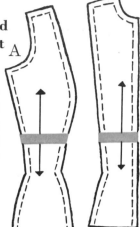

Lengthen (A) or shorten waist between waistline and bustline on the princess style the same as for other styles.

Correcting the shoulder slope

When correcting shoulder slope, pin pattern pieces together; then fold in and pin dart across back or front (A). Leave alteration pinned in place, but unpin pattern pieces (B).

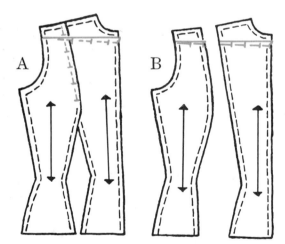

Adjustments for the full bust

Adjustment for the fuller bust can be made in two ways: lengthen the waistline; then sew in a bust dart (A). Or, lengthen front waist the necessary amount; then slash the side gore at the bustline to the side seam. Spread the slash at the front seam for the amount the waist has been

lengthened. This has the same effect as a dart. It gives a deeper slope at the side gore toward the shoulder, more cupping for the bust (B).

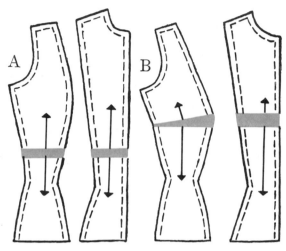

Increasing the waistline

To increase the waistline, additions can be made at the outside seam for a small amount (A). If a larger amount is to be added, slash in on the waistline mark, then slash toward the armhole and swing open the needed amount (B). The same amount can be added toward the hipline. The waistline can be decreased by the same method (C).

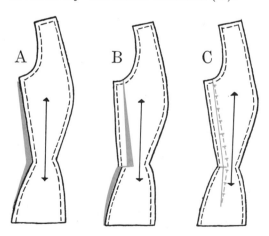

Kimono sleeve

The same alteration used for adjusting the shoulder of a set-in sleeve can be used to narrow or widen the shoulder of the kimono sleeve. The sketches show adjustments needed.

On the shoulder line of the kimono sleeve, mark the finished width of your shoulder. Take this measurement from your basic pattern. If you need to adjust your pattern for square shoulders, fold the dart from under the neck toward this mark.

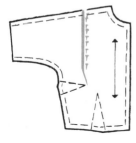 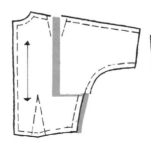

Narrow shoulders   Wide shoulders

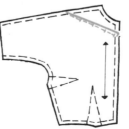 

Square shoulders

Lengthen or shorten the waistline of the dress in the same way as you did on the basic muslin.

If you are adjusting the pattern for a sloping shoulder, slash from under the neck toward this mark.

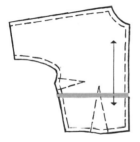 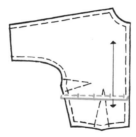

Long waistline   Short waistline

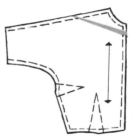 

Sloping shoulders

Eliminate the bustline fullness in the same manner as on the basic muslin, with a tuck running the entire length of the bodice. To increase for a larger bust, follow the instructions given for increasing for a full bust on the basic pattern.

To increase the pattern for the broad back, follow same instructions given on the basic pattern. If front shoulder needs to be narrowed, but not the back, increase size of back dart to fit front. This adjustment will give a more comfortable fit.

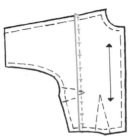 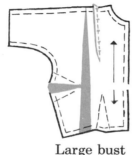

Small bust   Large bust

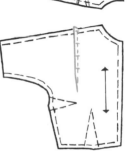

Broad back

Cutting your dress

During an informal question-and-answer period at a sewing clinic, a woman in the audience commented:

"I sew beautifully; my fitting is excellent; the finished dress looks as though it were made by a professional—but how do I find the courage for the first cut in the fabric!"

If this is the reaction of an experienced sewer, it isn't hard to imagine how a beginner feels when she is ready to cut her dress. Once there may have been a reason for this fear —when a sewer couldn't be sure her dress was really going to fit, and was afraid of ruining several yards of beautiful, and often, expensive fabric.

With today's professional ways of altering a pattern and fitting a dress before it is even cut out, there's no need for concern about the fit of the finished garment.

Using the new method, you fit yourself first with a basic muslin made from a commercial pattern. All fitting and alterations are done on this muslin. Then adjustments are transferred to the pattern before your garment is cut. After you learn to use this basic muslin, you will find that fitting is almost eliminated. A garment can be cut and sewed with only minor adjustments. These basic adjustments apply to all garments you make—suits, coats, dresses, or separates. Because of its importance, it's advisable to read carefully the information on fitting and pattern adjustment before making a dress.

From the pattern envelope choose the style or view that you plan to make. Check the amount of yardage you will need. (Even though you may be working with a smaller pattern to give you a smaller armhole, use the yardage guide for your bust size.) Yardage will also depend on the style, width of fabric, and whether the fabric you choose has a nap.

Remove from the envelope only the pattern pieces for the style you are making. This eliminates the possibility of cutting unnecessary pieces. Smooth the pattern by hand. Only an old pattern, carelessly folded, must be pressed with an iron before re-using. Neat sewing habits save work.

If you are using a basic muslin as described, check your fitted muslin against the pattern pieces, and make the necessary pattern alterations.

Don't fit pattern pieces over the muslin. Measure and transfer the muslin alterations to the dress pattern.

Know these pattern markings

All commercial patterns are printed, which makes them easy to use. Read all the information printed on the pattern piece itself and you can't go far wrong in making up a dress.

If this is your first experience with a printed pattern, here are some of the markings you'll want to study.

Margins

All patterns have an extra margin that extends beyond the actual cutting line of the pattern. This is a safety margin to insure correct size. When patterns are printed, they are piled up many ply deep and cut out with a knife. If patterns were actually trimmed along the cutting line, a natural shifting of the thin paper might cause some of the pattern to be cut away. By trimming well outside the actual line, the cutters leave a margin of safety on the pattern.

Cutting line

It isn't necessary to cut off this margin before you cut your dress. When you lay out your pattern pieces, lap the margin so that the cutting lines come together. When you cut the dress, follow the actual cutting line and the margin will drop away.

This extra margin is actually an advantage, because the fabric shifts less when cut through the paper.

Before you cut, many alterations can be marked on the pattern margin in red pencil. This saves you time and gives you a permanent record of the adjustments made.

Seam allowance line

Inside the cutting line is a broken line printed all around the pattern. This is the seam allowance which shows where to sew the pieces together. All patterns have a ⅝-inch seam unless a design detail calls for a wider or narrower one, in which case the pattern will be marked. Follow the correct seamline exactly.

Fold line

Some pattern pieces may show a lighter line, or a single line on one side. Printed along this line will be instructions such as "Center front or back, place on fold," or "Place on fold." This indicates that the pattern piece is half of a complete piece, such as a back or front bodice. Usually the piece is cut on the lengthwise fold of goods or parallel to the selvage, unless the pattern specifies otherwise.

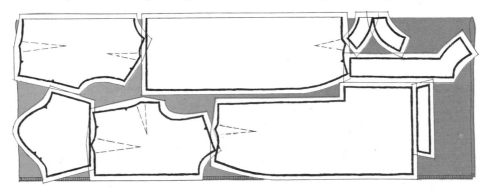

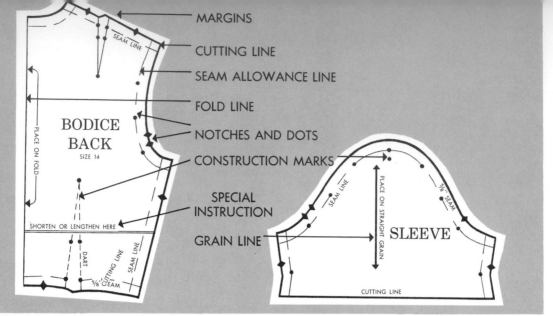

Labels in figure:
- MARGINS
- CUTTING LINE
- SEAM ALLOWANCE LINE
- FOLD LINE
- NOTCHES AND DOTS
- CONSTRUCTION MARKS
- SPECIAL INSTRUCTION
- GRAIN LINE
- SEAM LINE
- BODICE BACK SIZE 14
- PLACE ON FOLD
- SHORTEN OR LENGTHEN HERE
- DART
- CUTTING LINE
- SEAM LINE
- 5/8" SEAM
- SLEEVE
- PLACE ON STRAIGHT GRAIN
- SEAM LINE
- 5/8" SEAM
- CUTTING LINE

Grain line

Every commercial pattern piece has an arrow or a heavy line to indicate the grain line. Place the arrow on the straight thread of the fabric. It's very important to follow the grain line because it is often used to give a special hang to a skirt or other part of a garment.

The entire style can be spoiled if the grain line is ignored. You'll find printed along this mark "Cut on lengthwise of goods," which means the up-and-down grain, or parallel to the selvage.

If the piece can also be cut on the cross-grain without spoiling the style of the dress, the pattern instructions will read "Cut on lengthwise or crosswise of goods."

Collars, cuffs, yokes, pockets, and other trimming details can usually be cut on either grain unless the pattern indicates otherwise. This is especially true with striped fabrics, since use of a stripe on the cross-grain can serve as a trimming.

On fabrics such as satin or napped fabrics, a difference in shade occurs if pieces are cut on a different grain. On these fabrics, cut all the pattern pieces on the same grain, regardless of pattern instruction.

Construction marks

Tucks, darts, pleats, and buttonholes, center front or back lines, placement of pockets or trimming details are all printed on the pattern.

Notches and dots

Carefully note the notches—triangular markings along the seamline edge of the pattern. They are numbered to help you correctly match and assemble corresponding pattern pieces.

Dot markings on a pattern indicate special points where seams are to be eased when joined—at the sleeve and armhole, for example. At the top of the sleeve there is a double dot or a large single dot to indicate where it joins the shoulder seam.

Special instructions

Special instructions on the pattern will explain additional marks. You'll find lines which indicate where shirring is to be used, or where alterations should be made. Special sewing instructions are also included.

After you have adjusted your pattern and become familiar with the markings, you are ready to concentrate on the fabric for your garment.

Follow the grain line carefully as you lay out your pattern.

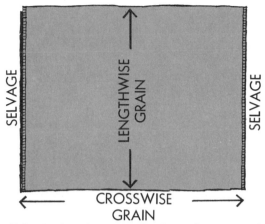

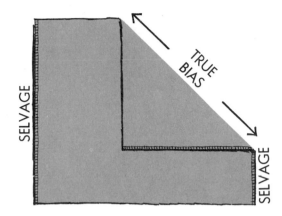

"Grain" refers to the lengthwise and the crosswise threads in your fabric: lengthwise grain runs parallel to the selvage; crosswise grain runs from selvage to selvage. Follow the grain line in cutting your fabric because it affects the hang of the garment.

You can find the true bias of your fabric by folding back a corner, with a crosswise thread parallel to the selvage or a lengthwise thread. The diagonal line formed is the true bias. A bias edge has the greatest stretch, ravels less than any other cut edge.

Selecting and preparing fabric for cutting

Much work goes into the sewing of a garment, so make your efforts worthwhile by using quality fabrics. You will find good material is easier to sew, and your monetary investment in quality will give you an added incentive to do good work.

The fabric industry has made rapid advances in the last ten years. Development of man-made fibers alone has done much to change the home sewing picture. The addition of new fibers continues; many fabrics combine several fibers—each contributing its own characteristics to the material.

Some of the new synthetics are blended with natural fibers to give added qualities to these old favorites.

New finishes have also been developed that make fabrics faster-drying, crease-resistant, soil- and stain-resistant, increase washability, and generally make fabrics easier to care for and more long-wearing.

This advancement in fabric development has brought a change in home sewing techniques. Old methods of preparing fabrics for cutting can be discarded. Modern fabrics are easier to use and give better wear.

Woolens

In the past, all woolens had to be sponged or shrunk before cutting. Now this is almost never necessary. Many woolen manufacturers have a special department to handle the production of "over-the-counter" fabrics—those made especially for the home-sewing trade.

Most better woolens are preshrunk before they are sold. Most manufacturers print on the wrong side or along the selvage of the fabric that it is sponged, ready to cut.

Be sure to check carefully when you buy fabric on sale. These fabrics may be from top manufacturers, but in many cases they are left over from the ready-to-wear trade. Fabrics sold for ready-to-wear manufacture are not sponged by the fabric-makers, as they are for home sewing. It's a good idea to check with the fabric buyer in a store, or test a piece of the fabric yourself at home to make sure it is already preshrunk.

If you should get a piece of material that hasn't been sponged, it is easy to have it done. Many stores provide this service to piece goods customers for a few cents extra per yard. Or, take the fabric to your dry cleaner who will put it through the press for a small fee.

Wool crepe should never be sponged. Some manufacturers guarantee their fabrics against shrinkage, and label them accordingly. Do not treat these fabrics in any way before cutting or the guarantee will be void.

Proper preparation of the fabric is vital in sewing. Before you cut your fabric, be sure it is on-grain. To get the straight grain, clip the selvage at the end and tear across the fabric. If it won't tear, pull a thread and cut along this line.

Now lay the fabric flat on a table

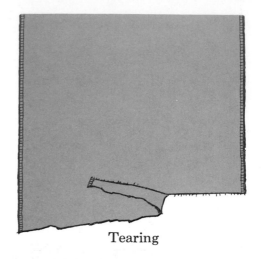

Tearing

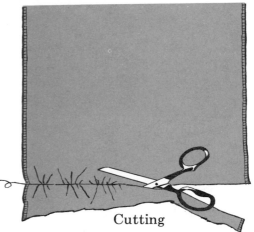

Cutting

and see if the ends are even. If one end looks shorter than the other, it has been stretched off-grain in the finishing. Have your dry cleaner stretch the fabric back in shape as he steams it for you.

If you prefer to do it yourself,

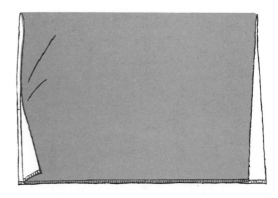

the fabric can only be straightened when damp. If it is only slightly off-grain, you can use a steam iron. If it is considerably off-grain, you will have to treat it as was formerly done to shrink wool.

Wet a sheet and wring it out. Put half the sheet lengthwise on a flat surface, and place half the lengthwise fold of wool on it.

Fold the other half of the sheet over the wool and fold the remainder of the wool on top of the sheet.

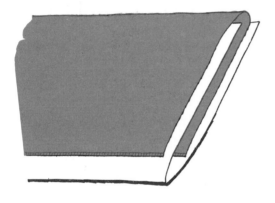

Roll it carefully with the sheet on the outside of the material.

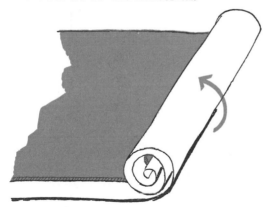

Let the roll stand for several hours, or until the moisture has penetrated the fabric. Unfold, smooth and stretch the fabric into shape or on-grain. Let it dry, and then press lightly with a steam iron. Your fabric is now properly treated, ready for cutting.

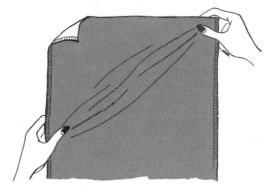

Linen

Although linens are often treated for crease-resistance, this finish does not necessarily control shrinking. It is always best to shrink linen before you cut it. This can be done by using a steam iron, or by pressing the fabric with a damp cloth.

To be sure the grain is straight, pull a thread across the end and cut on this line. *Linens can't be torn.* The texture of linen is such that the cut end can be straightened and made even just by smoothing the fabric with your hand.

Cotton

All cottons once had to be shrunk before cutting. Now, as with woolens, most cottons are processed especially for home sewing, so there is no need to worry about shrinkage in quality material. In addition, there are countless finishes used on cottons to make them easier to care for.

Inexpensive fabrics or special sale goods are the only exceptions. It is safer to preshrink these.

Also, check the grain line before you cut the fabric. Tear across the end of the fabric to see if it is straight. It is better to cut on-grain, but if you like a certain print, and find that it has been stretched off-grain in the finishing, it is still possible to use it. Most cottons have a resin finish, which won't wash out or dry clean away. It would be useless to dampen these fabrics and try to stretch them into shape. As long as the design of the print is not distorted by being off-grain, it is safe to cut your garment and sew it without worry.

In the past when a dress was cut off-grain, it lost its shape in washing or dry cleaning. This cannot happen when materials are treated with the resin finishes.

Shrinking cotton

If you buy an inexpensive or special sale cotton, it is a good idea to check it to see if it has been preshrunk. These fabrics are often leftover designer fabrics from the ready-to-wear trade. Since they were not intended for over-the-counter sales, there's a good chance they are not preshrunk. Many imported cottons are also not preshrunk.

To test a cotton fabric, take a small sample, measure it, then wash and let dry. If the sample is smaller when dry, the entire piece should be preshrunk. To shrink, leave the cotton folded as it comes off the bolt. Roll it up, forming loose, easy folds. Fill a basin or tub with lukewarm water. Let the cotton soak until it is wet through. Don't wring it out; squeeze gently to remove as much water as possible from it.

Hang it over a shower bar or a clothesline to dry. Smooth it with your hands as it hangs. If the fabric is off-grain, stretch it into shape when it is almost dry.

Iron it while it is still slightly damp. Ironing can be done while fabric is still folded on the lengthwise fold. Iron first on one side of the folded piece and then on the other to give the fabric a smooth finish. Your cotton is now ready to cut.

Cutting your fabric

After you have altered the pattern and prepared your fabric, you are ready to cut your dress.

In the pattern envelope you'll find an instruction sheet covering all phases of cutting and sewing the dress. There is a layout guide, planned by experts, according to size of pattern, various styles that can be made, and different fabric widths that can be used for this particular garment.

Check the layout that applies to the dress style and fabric you are using, and draw a circle around it.

Follow this layout carefully as you lay out all of the pieces before you begin to cut. If your table is not large enough to lay out all your fabric at once, pin as many pieces on the fabric as possible.

Then fold the material over and

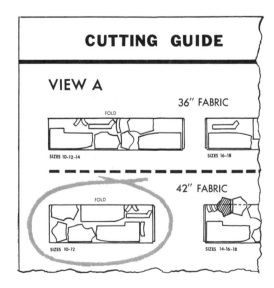

slide more fabric onto the table until all the pieces are pinned. As you cut out your pattern, unroll the folded material. If you have been sewing for a long time, you may have stopped following the "cutting guide" and developed a system of your own. In this instance, you still must be certain that you lay out all of the pattern pieces to make sure that there is enough fabric before you begin to cut your garment.

Grain line

As you pin the pattern to the fabric, be sure all of the pieces are on the straight of the goods. Check the line or arrow on the pattern that indicates the grain line. This line should run parallel to the selvage. To check, measure from the selvage to each end of the line with a ruler.

Fold line

A single line along the edge of a pattern piece indicates that it is to go on the fold of goods. Place the single line, not the margin edge, on the fold of the fabric.

Margins

You can overlap the extra pattern margins so that the cutting lines of the pieces almost meet. These cutting lines are accurate guides, so follow them exactly. As you cut through the paper, there is less chance of the fabric shifting, so this extra margin is actually an added aid to more accurate cutting of the pieces.

Cutting shears

Use the long, bent-handle shears for cutting, and cut with long, even strokes. Never lift the fabric as you cut. You will find it easier to cut if you keep your left hand flat on the fabric as you cut along the right-hand side of the pattern pieces.

Never use pinking shears to cut out a garment. They are not accurate for shaping around darts, armholes, necklines, or other intricate details. And, so much cutting would soon make them dull and difficult to use; save them for pinking seams.

OVERLAP THE MARGINS

USE CORRECT CUTTING SHEARS

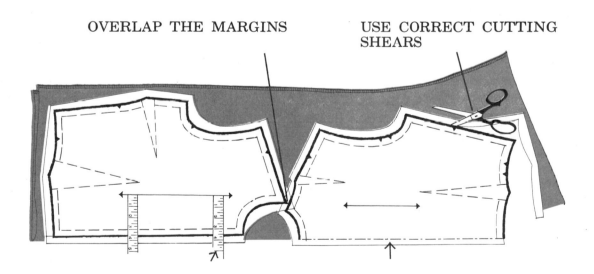

PIN PATTERN ON
STRAIGHT OF GOODS

PLACE SINGLE LINE
ON FOLD

Cutting stripes

There are four different types of stripes—length stripes, cross stripes, and diagonal stripes; the fourth is the one-directional version of any of the other three types.

The direction of a stripe is determined by the varying widths or colors which are used in it, and by the sequence in which the stripes are arranged on the fabric.

Length stripes

The peppermint or candy type of stripe can be cut in either direction and with little difficulty.

This stripe runs the length of the goods. When cutting a garment from a candy stripe, decide on the stripe to be used in the center skirt front and follow it in cutting the waist and skirt pieces.

Aside from centering, there is little matching to be done with this stripe.

If the skirt is gored, seams must "chevron;" where seams join, the stripes must come together in a point. To be sure seams chevron, check the notches where skirt seams join. Make sure seams fall on corresponding notches. When cutting to chevron, the point can be either up or down.

RIGHT   WRONG

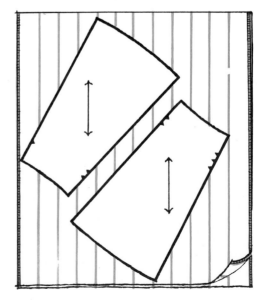

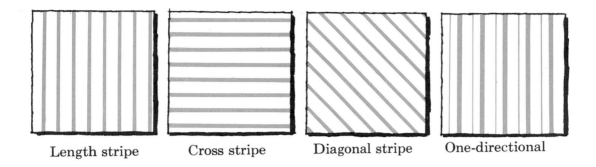

| Length stripe | Cross stripe | Diagonal stripe | One-directional |

Cross stripes

WRONG   RIGHT

When matching cross stripes, particularly watch the side seams, gores in the skirt, and armholes. The stripe must appear as one continuous line around the figure.

To match the side seam of the front and back waist, be sure that the notches are placed on a corresponding stripe of the fabric.

Also put the sleeve and armhole notches of the front and back waist pieces on a matching stripe when cutting. Lay skirt pieces so matching notches are also on the same stripe.

In cutting a cross-grain stripe, pattern pieces can be cut in either direction and interlocked to save on the amount of fabric needed.

Only when the cross stripe is one-directional should all your pattern pieces be cut in one direction to assure a matched look.

Diagonal stripes

Stripe cut to chevron

Diagonal stripes cannot be cut to give a chevron effect unless the fabric can be reversible, or is cut with the cross-grain against the up-and-down grain line.

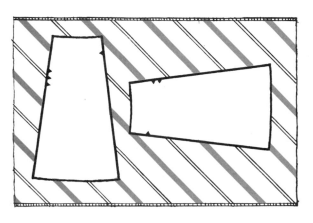

Cut pattern on diagonal stripe

This stripe is always printed on the fabric. Diagonal stripes are not often made by manufacturers.

A dress made in a diagonal stripe is usually cut so the entire garment is on the diagonal, with no attempt to chevron the stripes.

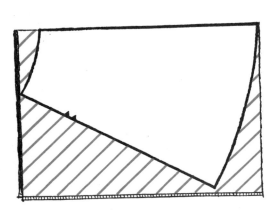

One-directional stripes

A pattern manufacturer usually illustrates a pattern in a stripe or plaid if the garment was designed for this type of fabric. In this case, the sweep of the skirt will be the same on all pieces so it can be chevroned. The style of the dress will have simple and uncluttered lines so that matching will not be difficult.

When you're using a one-directional stripe, it's better to select a dress with a seam down the center back and front, or one that can be cut with such seams without spoiling the style.

It is sometimes difficult to tell whether a stripe is one-directional when the fabric is in several colors and has graduated widths of stripes.

An easy test is to fold the fabric lengthwise, then turn back one side of fabric across the end. If it is a balanced stripe, all the stripes on the upper fold will match those on the under side. If they do not match, it is a one-directional stripe.

To match these stripes, the fabric must be folded on cross-grain. Pieces cannot be cut on a lengthwise fold, thus there is the need for a pattern style that has the seams front and back, or one that can be cut with such seams. Add a ⅝ inch seam allowance at fold line of the pattern.

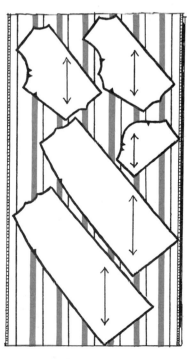

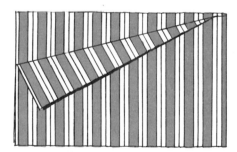

Balanced stripe

One-directional stripe

Cutting plaids

Balanced plaids

Even, or balanced, plaids are easiest to cut. They match on the crosswise or up-and-down plaid. It is sometimes hard to recognize a balanced plaid. To test, fold lengthwise and then turn back one side of the fabric at the end, as you do to test a stripe. If the identical plaids fall one on top of the other, the plaid is balanced on the cross-grain. Now fold the fabric on the cross-grain and turn back the top layer along the selvage. If the upper and under plaids match, it is a balanced plaid that can be cut in either direction.

Chevroning a skirt

Cut skirt pieces so the center of the back and front are on the same plaid as the bodice pieces. If the skirt is flared, seams should match around the skirt as well as up and down to form a chevron. To match the seams, be sure skirt notches are on the stripe around the skirt and on the same plaid running up and down.

WRONG

RIGHT

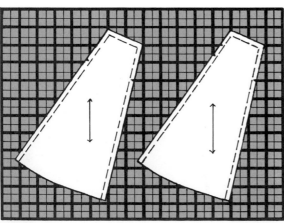

Cutting a dress

When laying out a pattern on a plaid, *always start with the front bodice.* This is the focal point of your dress, so matching must begin here. Always place the center front line of the dress on the center of a plaid stripe. If you don't, the dress will look off-balance, and the plaid will appear uneven, poorly matched.

Cut the center back on the same plaid, and shoulder seams will also usually match. Match the side seams of the front and back bodice pieces by placing matching notches on the same plaid stripe.

Match the sleeves by lining up front and back bodice notches and front and back sleeve notches on matching plaid stripes.

If the front bodice has an underarm fitting dart, it is sometimes impossible to have the underarm seam match below this dart. It is more important to match the top of the bodice so that the sleeves can also be matched. Poor matching here is much more distracting to the eye than it is at the underarm seam.

WRONG

RIGHT

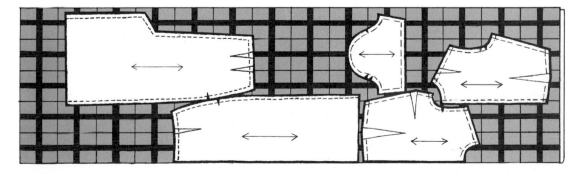

One-way, one-directional plaids

This term is not meant to confuse. A one-way, one-directional plaid is one that balances across, but not up and down; or, it may balance up and down, but not across.

If it is one-directional across, but balances up and down, fold the fabric on the cross-grain so that the plaid on the top layer matches the plaid on the under layer. Then all pieces can be cut on the double, and your plaid will match.

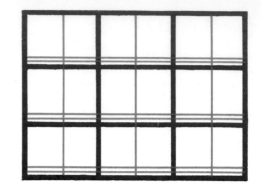

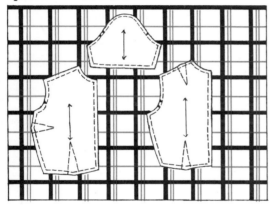

Choose a style that opens, or has a seam, down the front or back. The bodice should be in two pieces if the plaid is to balance correctly.

If the plaid is balanced across, but is one-directional up and down, cut all pieces on the length fold as usual, but lay all the pieces in one direction, as you do when cutting a garment in a one-directional print.

Tips on matching sleeves

Sleeveless dress

On a sleeveless or a drop-shoulder dress style, it is better to match at the underarm seam, since there is no sleeve set in.

Kimono sleeve

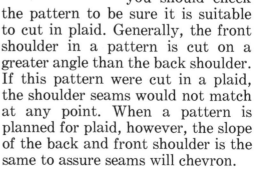

When a dress has a long kimono sleeve, it is important that the shoulder seam chevron along the top. This is why you should check the pattern to be sure it is suitable to cut in plaid. Generally, the front shoulder in a pattern is cut on a greater angle than the back shoulder. If this pattern were cut in a plaid, the shoulder seams would not match at any point. When a pattern is planned for plaid, however, the slope of the back and front shoulder is the same to assure seams will chevron.

One-directional, two-way plaids

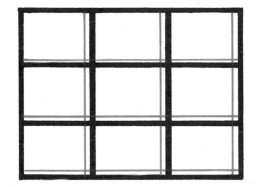

These plaids are difficult to cut unless the fabric can be used on either side. Again, it is better to choose a style in which none of the pieces are cut on a fold. It is better to cut out individually all the pieces that make up half of the dress. Then, reverse the fabric and cut the other half by matching to the original.

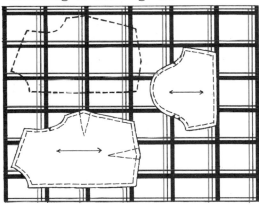

Bodice with center seam

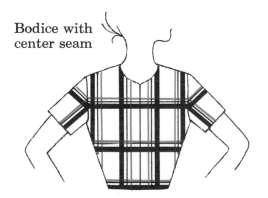

Follow all the rules for matching plaids. This type can also be cut so the plaid is continuous across the front of the garment in the same sequence as across the fabric design. This can only be done, however, on the most simple type of dress where little piecing is necessary.

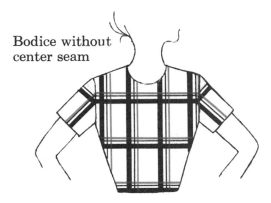

Bodice without center seam

Tricks in sewing plaids

There are many sewing and fitting techniques that can make plaids look like something they're not.

Here's a trick for making up a plaid dress: Suppose you have a piece of black-and-blue plaid, and you want your dress to look predominantly dark. Cut the dress with the black stripe running down the center front and it will look primarily black, even though the fabric has equal amounts of black and blue.

If you want the dress to look predominantly blue, then make the blue plaid stripe the center of your dress.

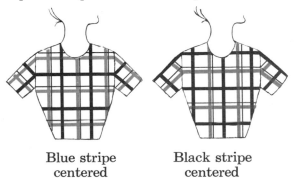

Blue stripe centered   **Black stripe centered**

Cutting prints

One-directional prints

Some prints, plaids, stripes, and checks must also be cut one way, like a nap fabric.

Always examine your print fabric to see how the motif is repeated. If there is a definite pattern, such as a sprig of flowers with the design all pointing the same way, then it is a one-directional print and must be cut like a nap fabric.

When you buy any of these printed materials, consult your pattern guide for yardage and buy the amount required for nap fabric.

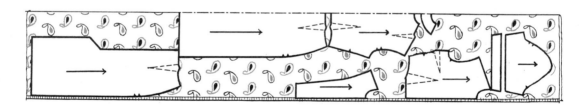

Allover prints

When the print you select has an allover effect, with no definite design or direction, you can cut and handle it like plain fabric.

Or, a print may have a definite design, but if it is printed with the motif repeated in either direction, it can be cut like a plain-colored fabric, with the pattern pieces going either way.

Large scattered prints

It isn't necessary to cut large scattered prints so that the same large motif is in a corresponding place on the dress.

Use a great deal of care to avoid getting all of the design motifs on one side of the garment and none on the other. The preferred method for cutting these large scattered prints is called "spotting the print;" areas of color or motif balance each other on the dress, but are not matched exactly. This eliminates the waste of material that occurs when you try to match large prints on a garment.

Be certain that you place the design for the most pleasing effect. Take care that large designs do not fall in ludicrous positions. For instance, cut a flowered pattern so that one large flower is at the shoulder on one side, and another is just under the bust on the other side.

Also, watch placement of the design on the skirt. Try to avoid running the pattern all around the skirt at the same level.

On side panels, place motif at hip level, but on the front panel, move it toward the hemline.

Use a method called "spotting the print" to balance color and motif as you cut large designs.

WRONG   RIGHT

Cutting special fabrics

Some material requires special care in cutting. It isn't likely that you will choose one of these for your first sewing attempt, but, as you continue to sew, you may want to use some of them. Learn about these fabrics now and you'll have no fear of trying them. It's more fun to sew when you can make any style and use any fabric you want for greater variety.

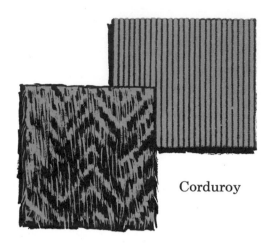

Corduroy

Nap fabrics

These fabrics have a definite surface texture, and must be cut in one direction to avoid shading.

Velvets, corduroys, and velveteens have a raised nap and must be cut with the nap running up toward the top of the dress.

To find which way the nap runs, rub your hand along the surface of the material. If it ruffles up like an animal's fur, then the nap runs up in that direction, and all pattern pieces must be cut that way.

If you should cut your pieces in both directions by mistake, the garment will appear to be cut from fabrics of different colors.

When all of the pattern pieces are cut with the nap running up, you get the full, rich color; this is called "looking into the nap."

Wool fleece

Other nap fabrics such as panne velvet, wool broadcloth (or facecloth as it is sometimes called), fleeces, textured wools, camel's hair, suedecloth—in fact, all other types of nap or surface fabrics—are cut with the nap running down.

Again, cut all of the pattern pieces one way to avoid shading. These fabrics are cut with the nap running down so that the fabric will wear better, and will never look roughed up from sitting or moving.

Be sure pieces, such as cuffs and yokes, usually cut on the crossgrain, are also cut with correct nap.

Fabrics with a definite surface texture must be laid out and cut in one direction to avoid shading and to get full benefit of color.

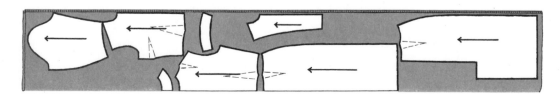

Jersey

Wool jersey comes in a tubular piece that is economical to cut out, since both sides are fold edges. It does not need to be sponged or shrunk before cutting, and is treated to prevent stretching of the length so that it is easy to work with and sew.

The fold edge of jersey is often stretched or twisted slightly in the finishing process, and is hard to straighten or press out. It's best not to place this line conspicuously down the front or back of a dress. When you have pattern pieces to cut on the fold, be sure to refold the jersey so that you are always cutting on a fresh fold of the cloth.

Some new jerseys have a nap, or are textured. To be safe, always cut jersey with all pieces going in one direction.

Heavy wools

Here's a tip that will help you cut heavy wools or fleeces. No matter how carefully you smooth out a wool fabric, the pieces tend to stick together. After you have cut all your pattern pieces, unpin the pattern and shake out the cut pieces. Put them together again as they were and re-pin the pattern in place.

You will find, in many cases, that the under piece is slightly larger than the upper piece. Recut them so that both pieces are even.

Plaids

Never cut a dress in plaid or check if your pattern specifically warns against it. Some styles must be completely avoided because the designs will not match. For instance, princess-line dresses are, as a rule, too cut up to match. Any style with a great deal of detail is usually a poor choice for a plaid fabric.

Yokes, pockets, collars, and other trimming details can sometimes be cut on the bias. This eliminates the need to match and also gives an interesting trimming effect.

No yardage is shown on a pattern for cutting plaids, since it is impossible to know how large the "plaid repeat" on the fabric will be. The safest rule is to allow the amount of fabric shown for nap fabrics, plus two additional "repeats of the plaid."

Checks

Any check that is $\frac{1}{4}$ inch or smaller does not have to be matched in cutting. On larger checks, follow the rules for cutting plaids.

Checks can also be one-directional, so watch carefully. A one-directional check is usually determined by the placement of color.

Trimming details cut on the bias

Assembling the dress

Now the fun of sewing really begins as you start to assemble your dress. Today you can learn to sew the fast, easy, professional way, yet still retain the quality associated with custom dressmaking. New equipment, quality fabrics, and accurate printed patterns all help to make sewing easier and more enjoyable.

Lay out dress for assembly

Now that you have finished cutting your dress, here's how to proceed. This system will help you now and in all your future sewing.

Mentally picture the parts of the garment that you are making. Lay out the cut-out pieces as they will be sewed together. First, lay out the front and back bodice as they will be joined. If there is a collar piece, put it at the neckline as it will be sewed. Next, find the facing pieces. Check to see where and how these will be used. If there is a pocket detail, place it in proper position. Proceed in the same way as you lay out the skirt pieces

as they will be assembled on the dress.

You'll find this eliminates the confusion of unrelated pattern pieces, and gives you a clear picture of how the entire garment goes together.

Now you're ready to mark and sew

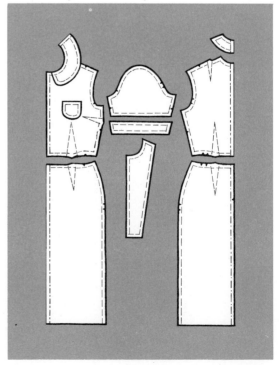

the cut-out pieces. It's no longer necessary to baste or tailor-tack before sewing. Tailor-tacks were one of the most time-consuming of the old methods, and were not even particularly accurate.

Marking notches

Here's how to put your garment together so quickly that you won't need markings that must last for a long time. The new way to mark notches is by simply slashing from the center of the notch toward the point for about ¼ inch. This gives enough of a mark to work from, and is fast to do. You can also cut out on the notch, as the pattern shows,

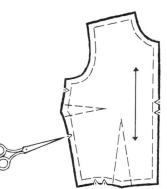

although this takes unnecessary time and material. Be sure that you mark every notch. They are printed on the pattern to help you match the pieces and join them correctly.

For example a princess-line dress has notches above and below bust-line on front and side front gores. The notches are important because this side gore is differently shaped than the front one, and it has fullness to be eased at a certain point. By matching notches,

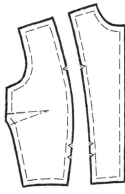

fullness at the bust will be correct.

Marking darts and tucks

Darts, and other design and construction details, such as tucks, shirr-

ing, and pleats, are printed on the pattern pieces. They should all be marked on the fabric before the pattern is removed from cut-out pieces.

First, mark the darts. Two methods have replaced tailor-tacks; both are faster and more accurate.

Tracing wheel method

One method of marking darts is done with a tracing wheel and carbon. To mark fabrics that have been cut with wrong sides together, fold the carbon paper with the carbon sides out. Slip it between the two layers of fabric and, with a tracing wheel, mark the shape of the dart.

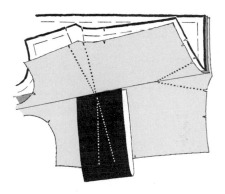

When the wrong sides of the fabric are on the outside, slip one sheet of carbon paper under the fabric and another on top of the fabric, under the pattern piece. Carbon sides of the paper should be placed against the fabric. Again, use the tracing wheel to mark the darts.

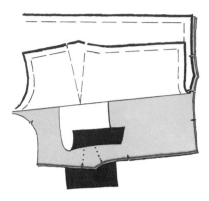

Pin and chalk method

Mark the dart by a pin at the point of the dart, and on either side at about 2-inch intervals. In pinning, put the pin in and out only once with the head close to the pattern. At the end of the dart where it finishes in the seam, clip in for about ¼ inch.

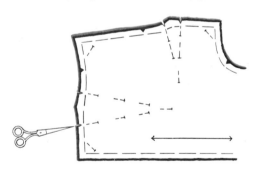

Mark all darts this way. Now remove the pattern from the material by pushing the head of the pin through the tissue and sliding the pattern off the point of pin and fabric.

The pins remain in the cut-out material, and you're ready to mark the darts for sewing. It doesn't matter which side of the material is on the outside when you mark it. If the right sides of the material are together, take your tailor's chalk and mark along the line of pins on the wrong side of the cut-out pieces; then

you can remove the pins from fabric.

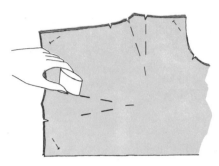

If the wrong sides are together, without removing the pins, fold back one piece and mark with chalk at the points where the pins still hold the fabric. Once the material is marked, remove the pins and the darts are ready to be sewed. The chalk mark is clearly visible on the fabric, and indicates proper shaping of the dart.

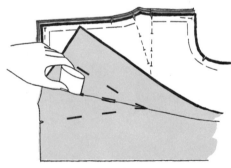

Functions of the dart

The dart has a vital function in dressmaking. It is more than just a means of fitting; it also helps create the contour of the fashion silhouette.

First, consider the dart in fitting. Here are some tips that will help you make your garment fit better.

When sewing in a dart that finishes

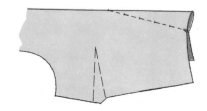

to a point, be sure to taper it gradually toward the point. If not sewed correctly, a puff forms at the point of the dart which even pressing will not smooth away. If you find it hard to sew the dart so that it tapers to a point, draw a straight line with your tailor's chalk from the wide part of the dart to the point, and follow this line as you sew.

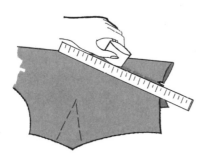

In marking darts used to create a style silhouette, be very careful to mark the actual printed dart line on the pattern pieces.

Sometimes the dart is planned to give a concave line to a dress; at other times it may give a convex line. Mark these darts with the tracing wheel, rather than tailor's chalk and pins, to be sure of getting proper shaping. A rounded hipline can be created by using a convex dart; a flat diaphragm look is made with a concave shaping of darts.

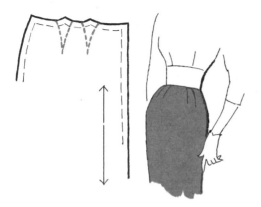

Convex dart

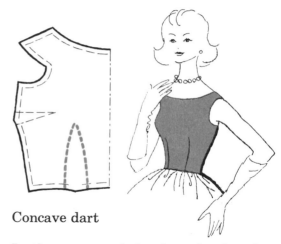

Concave dart

In the curve and shaping of a sheath dress, convex and concave darts are both used. After the darts have been stitched on a sheath or a dress without a waistline seam, they must be

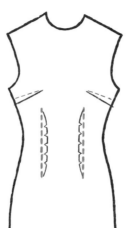

clipped at waistline point to help keep the garment from wrinkling at the waist.

One rule of the professional dressmaker is to press all the seams and darts as you sew them. You'll find a special section on "Pressing Tips" on page 53.

Marking trimming details

The pattern also indicates placement of the pockets and other trimming details. Mark them on the dress fabric with your tailor's chalk.

Bound buttonholes are the only details that you do not mark now. In the Creative Sewing Book on Professional Sewing Tips *you'll learn the easy way to make them, and a fast and accurate method for marking them. This book also contains professional tricks in finishing a dress that eliminate the "loving hands at home" look.*

Shirring

When shirring is used, your pattern will be marked with two lines, indicating where it goes. Mark for shirring as you do for notches; that is, slash the seam for about ¼ inch at either end of the gather lines.

The easy way to shirr is by machine. Simply enlarge the stitch on your machine, loosen upper tension, and stitch two rows about ¼ inch apart. Make first row on seam allowance line. As you begin shirring, sew between slashes on right side of fabric. Shirr by easing fabric along on bob-

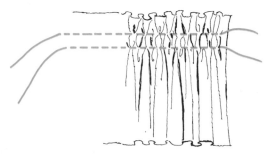

bin thread. If shirring is very full, with a lot of fabric to be eased in, use nylon thread in bobbin. It is stronger and less likely to break.

Use at least two rows of stitching when you gather, so the fabric will not roll and will be easier to handle. The advantage of gathering by machine is that it can be done rapidly, and the gathers will be even.

Another tip: Dressmakers usually suggest the largest stitch on the machine for gathering. On soft, sheer fabrics, such as chiffon, however, gathers will be finer if you use a smaller stitch. Try to gauge stitch size by weight and texture of fabric used.

Sometimes the style of the pattern requires additional rows of gathers. You can sew as many rows as you like by machine. The trick is to ease all rows on the bobbin threads at once.

Sew your dress in sections

Now you're ready to assemble your dress in sections. Lay out your cut-out pieces to get a visual picture of how the dress goes together.

Make the skirt first, since it is the easiest to sew. Take the skirt a piece at a time, and make sure all notches, darts, tucks, or shirring are marked before you remove the pattern. Start with either the front or back piece, but *only remove the pattern as you are ready to sew.*

Sew all tucks, darts, gathers, or other detail while the garment is still in pieces and easy to handle and sew. After you have sewed the detail on each skirt piece, you will be ready to sew up the seams.

If you have worked from a fitted basic muslin, as discussed on page 8, you can assemble your skirt to this point and be sure of a good fit.

Pinning is much faster and easier than the old way of basting all the seams. Match all notches on your skirt seams and pin as follows.

Pin skirt pieces with the point of the straight pin toward the hem of the skirt, the head toward you, placing pins parallel to the seam. When you pin the dress seams together, place pins ⅝-inch from the edge of the fabric. As you sew,

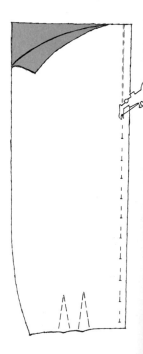

the pins will serve as a guide line for the proper seam allowance. Place pins as close together as you like.

As you sew, you can remove the pins quickly and easily, since the heads are toward you. Sew from pin to pin for a straight seam.

Let the skirt hang while you put the bodice together.

Mark and sew all tucks, notches, shirring, or other details. If the dress opens down the front, mark the center front with a basting line so it is clearly defined at the try-on.

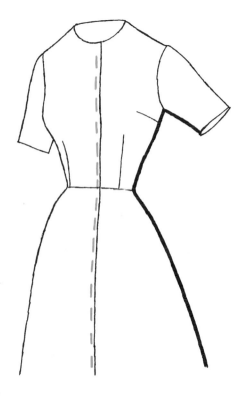

Pockets and other trimmings can be made at this point and pinned in place on the dress for the try-on. Your pattern instruction sheet shows details. (See Creative Sewing Book on *Professional Sewing Tips* for making pockets, collars, other detail.)

It's a good idea to check these trimming details to be sure they are becoming and in the most flattering

place for your figure before you sew them permanently.

You can also sew up the sleeves. Mark the darts at the elbow for a three-quarter or long sleeve. It's safe to sew in the darts if you have checked sleeve length and placement of the darts from a fitted basic muslin, as described on page 23. If you are not using a basic muslin, then baste the darts for the try-on, and check to see that they fit correctly at the sleeve elbow.

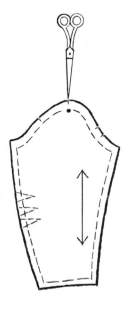

Next, mark the circle at the top of the sleeve with a slash of the scissors as you do for a notch. This indicates where the top of the sleeve matches shoulder seam. Also sew up the underarm seam of dress.

If you are uncertain about how to put some of the pattern pieces together because of a certain style detail, turn to the instruction sheet in your pattern envelope. It gives you explicit directions for making and assembling every detail of the dress.

As each of the seams is stitched, pink it and press it before any cross seams are sewed. It's a good idea to invest in a pair of pinking shears. They are timesaving, give a neat finish to seams, and help keep the fabric from raveling.

There are several ways that dress seams can be finished, depending upon the weave and weight of the fabric. Here are a few types for use on various fabrics. Whatever finish you use, do it before you sew cross seams.

Seam finishes for your dress

Pinked seams

Pinked seams are used most often. Pinking is fast, and provides an adequate finish on a firm fabric. It prevents fraying and gives a neater appearance. Special pinking shears are also made that cut a scalloped edge. Pinking shears can also be used to cut decorative edges, as well as for simple finishing of garments.

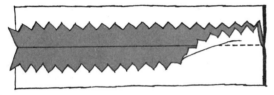

Pinked

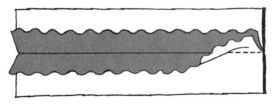

Scalloped

Stitched-edge seams

If the fabric has a slight tendency to ravel, stitch along the edge of the seam after it has been pinked. The stitched-edge seam looks neat, and the extra stitching helps to keep the fabric from raveling.

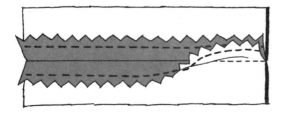

Pinked edges can also be stitched on a zigzag sewing machine, if you have that type. Or, seams can simply be finished with a zigzag stitch—a quick, easy finishing method.

On lightweight fabrics that ravel excessively, turn the raw edge under about $\frac{1}{4}$ inch, and stitch close to the turned edge for a neat seam.

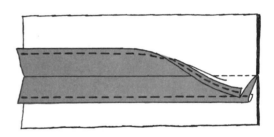

Bound edges

It is better to bind the edges on heavy fabrics that have a tendency to ravel. Use seam binding or silk bias binding. Crease the binding in the center, place it over the seam edge and stitch along the edge of binding, through the three thicknesses of fabric.

The bound-edge type of seam finish is also used on jackets and coats that are unlined.

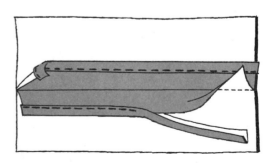

Hand-finished seams

On very sheer fabrics, turn the seam edge under and overcast by hand to prevent the fabric from raveling.

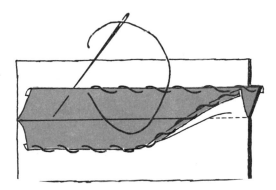

On firmer fabrics, the raw edge can be overcast along the raw seam, or can be pinked and then overcast.

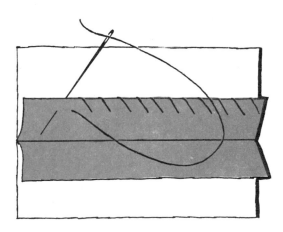

If seams are to be pressed to one side, overcast both edges together for a neat finish.

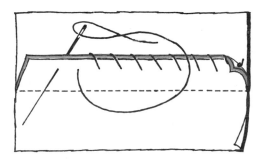

Pressing tips

A good rule to follow for professional-looking clothes is to "press as you sew." As you finish sewing each section of your dress, press it. Here are some rules for you to follow in pressing all details on your dress. They'll improve the appearance and make sewing much easier.

Darts

Darts are used to mold, shape, or fit. It's important that a dart keep the contour you have sewed into it, so never press it on a flat board. Slide a tailor's mitt onto the end of your sleeve board, with the cushion part on top of the board.

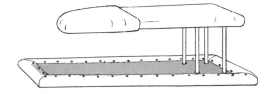

When you press darts, mold them over the cushion. For best results, always place the point of the dart toward the round end of the cushion.

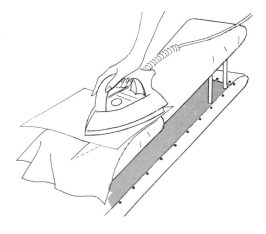

How to press darts

Always press skirt darts toward the center of the skirt. Press waist darts toward the center of the bodice. Press bust darts down. The shoulder darts on a dress are pressed toward the center, and the elbow darts are always pressed down.

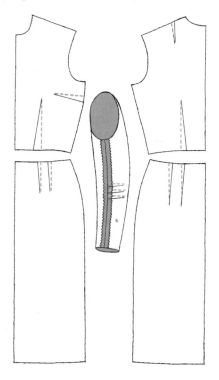

How to press seams

Usually, all straight seams should be pressed open unless the pattern indicates otherwise. (Sometimes, a design detail calls for special handling.) Press both edges of the seam together along the stitching line; then open and press flat. This makes the seam easier to press, and gives a smoother seam. Press hip or other shaped seams over a tailor's mitt or on a tailor's ham. (This equipment is especially useful for tailoring coats and suits.)

When a seam is curved, such as a side seam that is contoured at the waistline, it should be clipped and

then molded over a tailor's mitt to give it shape. Place the mitt over the end of the sleeve board and press the seam carefully.

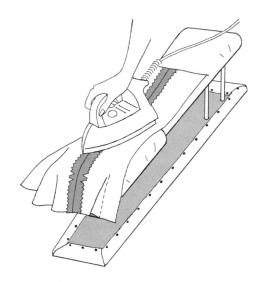

How to press shirring

Never press over shirring; it spoils the soft, puffy effect. Press shirred seams away from the shirring. For instance, on a dress with a dirndl skirt, press the seam up into the waist. If there is front shirring at the shoulder, press the seam toward the back of the garment.

Never press a shirred seam open.

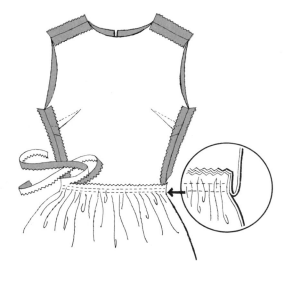

Finishing the dress

Setting in the sleeve

Many women have trouble setting in a sleeve, and believe it is because the patterns are cut too big. The sleeve is purposely cut larger than the armhole so that it can be molded and shaped to fit the top of the shoulder. Remember that the armhole seam should be well in on the shoulder for a correct fit. The sleeve must be capped to fit out smoothly over the top of your arm.

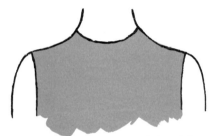

The capping is easy with this professional trick. Using the largest stitch on your machine, run two rows of shirring along the sleeve top from notch to notch. Put one row on the seam allowance line; run the second row ¼ inch closer to the edge.

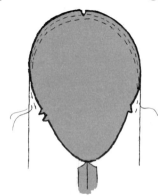

Sew on the right side of the sleeve

so bobbin thread is on the inside. Hold both bobbin threads. Ease the top of the sleeve along the thread so a cap, or cupping, forms. This cupping is eased in, rather than

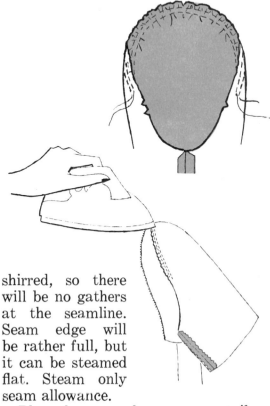

shirred, so there will be no gathers at the seamline. Seam edge will be rather full, but it can be steamed flat. Steam only seam allowance.

Place the seam edge over your tailor's mitt and press out the fullness with a steam iron, as you mold the top of the sleeve. The extra fullness in the sleeve is very little to ease in, when done with this method. (You'll find some fabrics handle more easily than others do.)

Here's another trick to get the sleeve in the correct armhole. Turn the sleeve and bodice right side out. Check the notches. Put your hand into the neck and out through the armhole of the bodice.

Hold the correct sleeve for that armhole by the underarm seam and bring it to the underarm of the armhole. Hold the two together while you turn the bodice inside out. The sleeve is now in the correct armhole, ready to be pinned. It can be pinned

and sewed easily and accurately—much better than by basting it.

Pin the underarm of the sleeve and bodice together. Pins should be parallel to the seam and on the seam allowance line. Next, match sleeve front and back notches to bodice and pin in the same way.

At top of sleeve, match slash mark (made when you originally marked the sleeve) to the shoulder seam and

pin. Key points are now all pinned. The rest of the sleeve eases into armhole, with pins placed parallel to the seams. Pin so head of one pin is touching point of the next. Sleeve should fit perfectly if it has been eased in enough. If there is still too much fullness, ease it in more with bobbin threads.

To sew, start at the underarm seam on the sleeve side. Sew from pin to pin. The heads of the pins will be toward you; you can easily remove them as you sew sleeve in armhole.

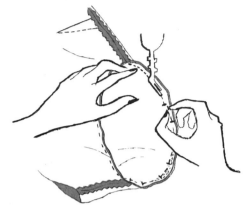

Pink or finish the seam allowance, then press lightly along the seam on the sleeve side to smooth fullness.

Now, turn the bodice of the garment to the wrong side and press the seam carefully over a tailor's mitt or ham. Never press an underarm seam. The rest of the armhole seam is generally pressed toward the sleeve.

Joining bodice and skirt

Now you are ready to permanently join the bodice and skirt. Turn the skirt wrong side out, and the bodice right side out. Drop the bodice inside the skirt and pin them together. Match the side seams, darts, center back and front seams, and any other parts of the skirt and bodice that should match. Sew them all together on the bodice side of the dress.

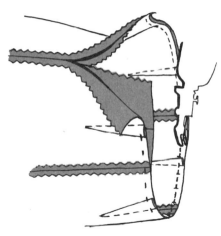

After the waistline is stitched, sew a seam binding just under the

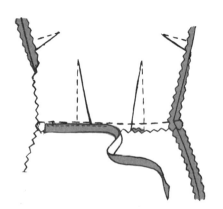

original waist seam on the bodice side. (Be sure the seam binding you select has been pre-shrunk before it is sewed.) The waistline will now be firm and not stretch.

Press the waistline seam down into the skirt in all cases except on a shirred or pleated skirt. Because of the bulk of the fabric, press these skirts with the seam toward bodice.

Open-front dress

On the coat-type dress, the joining at the waistline also takes care of the facing. Pin and sew the right side of the bodice to the right side of the skirt, starting from the center front line. Press the bodice facing back and pin in with the bodice front. Stitch the skirt and bodice together on the bodice side. After stitching,

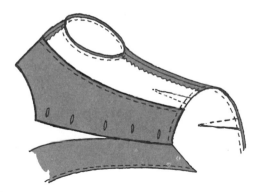

fold the skirt facing back so the bodice is between the facing and the skirt, and stitch. The facings will be securely held in place, and will

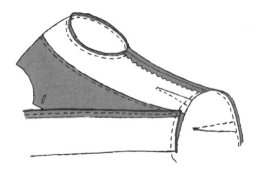

not require any hand-stitching.

Ribbon waistline

Grosgrain ribbon is the best finish for use in this waist. It keeps the waistline in place and also prevents stretching. Measure the grosgrain around the waist and cut it 3 inches longer. Turn back one end of the ribbon for ½ inch, and then fold under another ½ inch, and hem. Sew a hook on this end of the ribbon.

On the other end, turn under ½ inch and then fold under 1 inch. Hem this end, and sew the eye ½ inch in from the edge. Tack the center of the ribbon to the inside of the waistline so that the hook and the eye are at the opening of the dress.

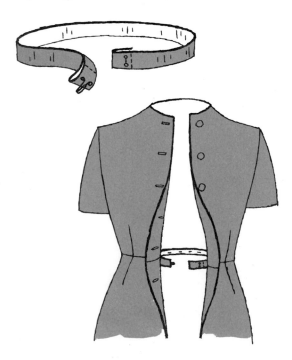

Plackets, loops

Dress placket

The left side of the dress has been left open for the zipper. It's easy to stretch this opening, since it is slightly bias. To prevent stretching, you can machine

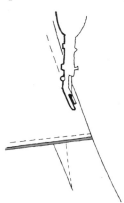

baste the placket seam closed, and then sew the zipper in while the seam is temporarily basted.

Placket opening should be as long as the metal part of the zipper.

Close the placket seam with a long stitch on the sewing machine.

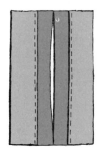

Check to be sure that the waistline seams are together. Press seam open. If seam allowance is less than $\frac{5}{8}$ inch, add a seam binding to extend.

Use the zipper foot on your machine when sewing in the zipper. Set the adjustable foot to the right-hand side of needle. Turn the dress inside out, with the back of

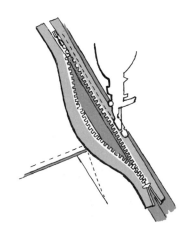

dress under front, right sides together.

Open the zipper and place it face down on the back seam allowance, with the teeth edge of the zipper at the seamline, the bottom stop of the zipper at the lower edge of the basting. Stitch from the bottom of the tape to the top. A woven guideline on the zipper tape indicates how far in you should sew.

Close the zipper and turn it face up. The back seam allowance turns under, making a narrow fold along the zipper. Shift the zipper foot to the left-hand side and stitch on this fold from one end to the other. Sew only through the seam allowance fold and the zipper tape.

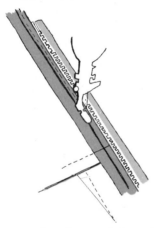

Next, turn the dress right side out. Press lightly along the seam.

Occasionally, if the waist is very small, there will be a slight puckering at the waistline. To correct it, turn the dress and rip in on the waistline seam to the placket closing, so it shapes correctly to the curve of the waist.

Turn the dress right side out and sew the zipper from the outside. The zipper automatically falls under the

front of the dress. Stitch across the top, down the side, and across the bottom of the zipper. Although you can't see the zipper, you can feel it under the seam. Rip out the basting stitch and the zipper is completed, sewed neatly in place.

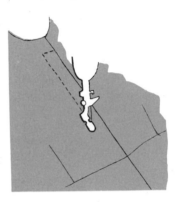

Sleeveless dress

This dress is easier to put on if you leave the left armhole seam open. Use a neckline-type zipper rather than a dress zipper. Allow $3/4$ inch clearance at the top. Sew the placket opening with a machine-basting thread, as you do with a dress placket. Follow the same instructions for putting in this zipper as for applying a skirt zipper.

Finish off the armhole facing to

the inside of zipper by hand. Sew a hook at the top of the zipper.

Back opening

In fine custom clothes the back zipper is put in with a lap seam, as on a sleeveless dress. This application can be done by hand or machine, depending on the type of fabric.

Facing

When the lap seam is used, the armhole and neck facing are finished differently. Trim and clip the facing seam. Turn to the inside, baste, and press the edge. Turn under the seam allowance on left facing and finish to the tape of the zipper. On the right facing, clip in on the seam allowance about ½ inch from the top, fold at an angle to clear the slider, and stitch to the zipper tape.

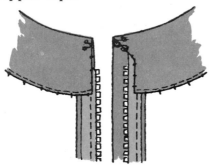

Slot or center application

This application does not conceal as well as the lap closure, but it is sometimes preferred in heavier fabrics because it is more flat. The style of the garment and weight of the fabric will affect the type of application you choose. Your choice will also depend on how inconspicuous the closure should be. It's advisable to know how to make both types.

The placket opening should be the length of the zipper from bottom of coil to the turned-up pull tab. Add

¼-inch for clearance at the top, plus a ¾-inch seam allowance.

Sew up the back opening with a machine-basting stitch, as you do for a side placket. If the seam allowance is less than ⅝ inch, extend the seams with seam binding. Be sure that waistline seams match.

Now press open the seam. Open

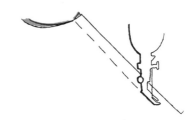

the zipper all the way and place it face down, on the extended seam allowance only. The teeth of the zipper should be along the seamline. Use the zipper foot on your machine and sew

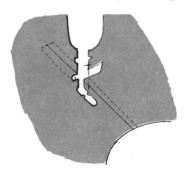

tape only to the seam allowance.

Sew from the bottom to the top along the woven guideline on the zipper tape. The top of the zipper should be ¾ inch from the edge.

Close the zipper, and turn the garment to the right side. On the right side, the zipper will be neatly in place under the center of seamline.

Stitch down one side of the seamline, across the bottom, and up the other side about ¼ inch away from the seam. Remove the basting line, press, and the zipper is finished.

On the unfinished neck or sleeve opening, the zipper should be placed approximately ¾ inch from the open edge of the neck or cuff, for a neat well-concealed closure.

Belt loops

If you want to use belt loops, make them at this point. They're usually placed at side seams, and can be crocheted or made with a blanket-stitch.

The belt loop should be made longer than the belt, so that it will easily slide through the loop.

Hand-crocheted belt loops

Use a knotted double thread about 2 feet long. Fasten it securely with short back-stitches in the side seam at the point where the top of the belt will be resting.

Pull the needle through the fabric to form the loop. Hold the thread with the needle in your left hand. Slip the loop over the thumb and first two fingers of your right hand.

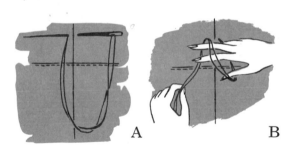

A   B

With thumb and forefinger, pick up the needle thread, pulling it through the first loop to form a new loop. Continue until you have a chain long enough for the belt to slip through. Finish the chain by slipping the needle through the last loop. Pull it tightly to form a knot. Sew to the side seam. Fasten securely on the wrong side of the garment.

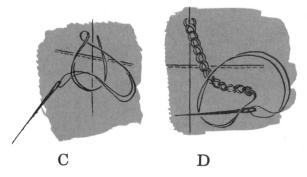

C   D

Hand-made belt loops

Bring the needle through from the wrong side above the belt line and take a stitch below the belt line.

Work back and forth two or three times. Then blanket-stitch over the strands of thread, drawing the stitches firm. Fasten the last stitch securely to hold firm.

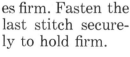
A

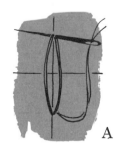
B

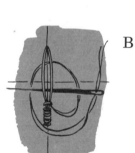

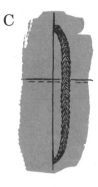
C

INDEX